Stand Up and Sing

Côr Cochion Caerdydd 1983–2003

a history and songbook

Beatrice Smith

Côr Cochion Caerdydd:

Wendy Lewis, Musical Director,
172 Pandy Rd, Bedwas, Caerffili, CF83 8EP
e-mail: wendy.lewis2@aladdinscave.net
website: www.corcochion.unisonplus.net

Cover artwork: Wendy Lewis

ISBN: 0 86243 694 X

Dinas is an imprint of Y Lolfa

Printed and published in Wales
by Y Lolfa Cyf., Talybont, Ceredigion SY24 5AP
e-mail ylolfa@ylolfa.com
website www.ylolfa.com
tel. 01970 832 304
fax 832 782

Contents

Author's Acknowledgements

I would like to thank everyone who has ever been a member of Côr Cochion Caerdydd, especially those who responded to my questionnaire, sent material, or took part in oral history interviews. Without them, this book could not have been written. Special thanks must go to the present Musical Director, Wendy Lewis, for her invaluable assistance and advice, and for taking on the boring task of proofreading the manuscript. Wendy Lewis, a noted artist, also did the artwork for the book cover.

In particular I wish to thank John C Abraham, the first Musical Director, who arranged eleven of the twenty songs in the book. He also modified the Wolfe Tones' arrangement of 'Only Our Rivers Run Free' and David Bedford's arrangement of Billy Bragg's version of 'The Internationalé'. I extend my gratitude to the deputy conductor, Ann Marie Fearon, for her arrangement of 'Songs of Freedom', based on the tune of the Max Boyce song, 'Hymns and Arias'. Miguel Heatwole of Sydney Socialist Choir arranged 'Co-operation Reigns'. Bronwyn Westacott arranged 'Watch Out'. 'Whole Wide World Around' was arranged by that well-known Socialist, Johann Sebastian Bach.

There could be no singing without the composers and lyricists. I wish to acknowledge and thank the following: Sergio Otega for words and music of 'El Pueblo Unido' (De Pie Cantar) and Cornelius Cardew for the English translation, 'Stand Up and Sing'; USA miners in the 1890s for the lyrics of 'Miner's Lifeguard', to the tune 'Life's railroad to Heaven' by Abbey and Tillman; Mal Finch for the words and music of 'Here We Go' ('Women of the Working Class'); Alex MacDaid for the original lyrics of 'Valley of Jarama', modified by Côr Cochion Caerdydd, to the tune of 'Red River Valley'; Holly Near for the words and Holly Near and John McCutcheon for the music of 'Watch Out' © 1983 Hereford Music (ASCAP), www.hollynear.com; the lyricist and composer of 'Asikatali'; Carlos Mejie Godoy for words and music of the Sandinista Hymn 'Adelante'; Côr Cochion Caerdydd members Helen Mary Jones, Wendy Lewis, and Beaty Smith for the words of 'Lords and Masters in their Mansions', music by Charles C Converse, 1868 for the hymn 'What a Friend we have in Jesus'; choir member David Hill for the lyrics of 'Jobs Not Bombs', music by John Hughes, Glan-dŵr, Abertawe, for the hymn 'Calon Lân'; Michael

MacConnell, words and music, 'Only Our Rivers Run Free'; Ewan McColl for 'Moving On Song'; the lyricist and composer of the Palestinian Anthem 'Mowtini – My Homeland'; Billy Bragg for new English lyrics to 'The Internationalé', music based on Degeyter; Jose Marti for words and music of 'Guantanamera'; Councillors Phil Bevan, John Taylor, and Lindsey Whittle (Plaid Cymru Review 1997) for the lyrics of 'All the Tories Failed in Wales', modified by Ann Marie Fearon, 2001; music John Hughes for the hymn tune 'Cwm Rhondda', tune 'Llantwit'; Paul Spencer for the lyrics of 'Co-operation Reigns' to the tune of 'I'm Leaving Tipperary'; Côr Cochion members for 'Songs of Freedom' – ten verses and still being added – from an idea from Ann Marie Fearon, who wrote the first four verses and arranged it to the tune of 'Hymns and Arias' by Max Boyce; choir member Sean Dudson for the words and music of 'Why Are We Victims?'; and Tom Glazier for the lyrics of 'Whole Wide World Around', music by Hans Hessler, arranged by J. S. Bach for the St. Matthew's Passion.

I have sought copyright clearance on the 20 songs in the book. If I have failed to contact a lyricist, composer, or arranger, I apologise. I also apologise if any information I have given is incorrect. Please don't hesitate to write and inform me of any errors or inaccuracies.

Beatrice Smith
August 2003

Chapter One

Stand up and Sing

Anti-Pinochet Demonstration, 11th September, 1983

On the tenth anniversary of the Pinochet dictatorship in Chile, September 1983, S.L.A.M. Cymru took two coaches from Cardiff to the London demonstration. On the way back one of the coaches broke down and everyone crushed into the same coach. We were on a high because of the successful demonstration and the crowded coach, and we wanted to sing. After 'Sospan Fach', followed by Tony Bianchi singing 'On Ilkley Moor B'aht 'At', we started singing Welsh hymns.

An old communist, Tommy Handley NSU, had been becoming progressively more angry as the choice of songs degenerated. He asked us to sing some socialist songs but we didn't know any. He sang, 'I'm the man, the very fat man who waters the worker's beer.' We were ashamed to admit that we had never heard of it.

Half a dozen of those protestors made a decision to meet regularly to learn socialist songs together. Their names have now become famous, or infamous. Ray Davies, Glynis Wisloki, Colin Matthews, Kay Davies and Tony Bianchi.

The first rehearsal was held a week later. It was a great success due to the musical skills of Tony and Diana Bianchi. We learned 'The Internationalé' in English, 'The Red Flag', 'I Don't Want Your Millions, Mister', and 'Halleluiah I'm a Bum'.

The choir name Côr Cochion Caerdydd was suggested by Lyn Mererid at the second rehearsal. It translates as Cardiff Reds Choir. We are many shades of red and represent a broad spectrum of the left; the Labour Party, Plaid Cymru (the Party of Wales), Trotskyists, Cymru Goch (The Welsh Republicans), Communists and Greens.

La Lucha International Festival.
La Lucha means 'the struggle' in Spanish.

VALLEY & VALE
SEL
GWERTHU MÂS
OUT

LA LUCH

THE VIDEO OF THE FESTI

"STRUGGLE IS THE HIGHEST SONG": HIGHLIGHTS FROM VALLEY & VALE'S "LA LUCHA" INTERNATIONAL FESTIVAL MARCH 1987 ON VIDEO

BRITAIN'S labour and democratic movement yesterday echoed the growing demand of the Chilean people that Pinochet's military dictatorship must go now.

Morning Star Reporter

This demand was voiced by over 5,000 demonstrators from a wide range of political, trade union and international solidarity organisations as they marched in driving rain through central London.

Addressing a rally later in Trafalgar Square, Chilean Communist Mireya Baltra was cheered as she declared that the Chilean people do not seek a dialogue with the Pinochet regime.

with the Pinochet regime. "Freedom and democracy can not be negotiated. Pinochet must leave now," demanded the former senator and Minister of Labour in Salvador Allende's Popular Unity government.

Ms. Baltra evoked the mass nature of the opposition to dictatorship by Chile's 11 million people, who are determined to make Pinochet's tenth year in power his last.

HUMAN RIGHTS

She described the nights of national protest as pots and pans are beaten, church bells rung and hundreds of barricades built and set alight as evidence of the burning discontent of

fore, as were numerous local and regional trade union bodies.

An effigy of the butcher Pinochet swinging on a scaffold was wheeled on a supermarket trolley, complete with bloody axe, and badges bearing swastika, CIA, ITT and dollar signs.

A new generation of Chilean democrats, children raised in British exile, chanted the Popular Unity slogan: "El Pueblo

ular Unity slogan: "El Pueblo Unido Jamas Sera Vencido." (The People United Will Never Be Defeated.)

Communist Party general secretary, Gordon McLennon, told the rally that comments on Central America by US Secretary of State Shultz indicated that the US is planning military intervention.

He pointed to the similarity between Mr. Shultz' comments and those of Henry Kissinger on Chile, at the time when the US was working to destabilise Salvador Allende's government.

Replying to organised heckling, Mr. McLennan received stormy applause as he charged: "Anyone who disrupts the unity of this demonstration is the

Anti-Pinochet Rally, September 11th, 1983.
The inspiration for the founding of Côr Cochion Caerdydd

STAND UP AND SING

Words & Music: Sergio Otega
English translation: Cornelius Cardew

1. De pie, can-tar, que vamos a triun-far, a- vanzan ya ban-deras de'uni- dad, y tu ven- dras, mar-
2. De pie, lu- char, el pueblo va'a triun- far, ser- a me- jor, la vida que vend- ra, a conquis- tar nues-
3. Stand up and sing, for victory will come, the banners of union as-semble in the sun, and you'll be there, be-
4. Stand up and fight, our hearts are all a-flame, a new life is coming to put the past to shame, your happi-ness is

chando junto'a mi, y'a-   si se- ra tu   canto'y tu ban- dera flore-   cer la luz de'un rojo' amane- cer, a-
tra felici- dad, y'en   un cla- mor, mil   voces de com- bate se'alza- ran, di- ran can- cion de liber- tad, con
side me on the march, and   then you'll see the   banners and the singing bursting   forth, the dawn whose coming we pro-claim, is
part of this our fight, a   thousand cries will   rise into a clamour that will   proudly sing, and we cannot be wrong, for

nun-cian ya la   vida que ven- dra
de-ci- sion la
red as blood, its
freedom is the   ~~rays set us a-~~ flame

patria vence- ra.

content of our song.   It's time for the people to   rise up in

struggle a-   gainst their o- ppressors and   shout out all to-gether:

El pueblo unido jamas sera vencido! The people united will never be defeated!

Chapter Two

Union Miners Stand Together

"A choir sang, most movingly, Socialist and Union songs."
George Melly, *Punch*, December 1984

During the 1984–85 strike of the National Union of Mine Workers, Côr Cochion Caerdydd became street performers. We have performed at union conferences, benefits, schools, castles, council chambers, guildhalls, working men's halls, public houses and the House of Commons, but we are happiest singing on the streets every week, usually outside the market in the centre of Cardiff. We raise awareness while raising money for hundreds of radical causes.

A school was packed to the doors at 8pm for the first benefit in South Wales for the miners in 1984. Unfortunately the crowd consisted totally of performers determined to sing depressing ballads. By midnight, two thirds of the audience had performed and departed. The other third were intent on performing until the caretaker threatened to lock them in.

The article by George Melly in the December 1984 edition of *Punch* was about a benefit held in Pen-yr-heol community centre, Caerffili, in the summer of 1984. Doom and gloom performers were banished and we all had a great time.

Paul Robeson Jr. toured South Wales in October 1986.

Following in his father's footsteps he supported the miners by speaking at a Justice For Miners benefit in Crynant. He also spoke at a Wales Anti-Apartheid Movement benefit in Butetown, Cardiff. The choir sang at both events and he presented us with a family photograph.

When we sang at a Justice For Miners benefit in Mansfield, we shared the platform with South African dancers who were in Britain to support the Anti-Apartheid Movement.

Arthur Scargill predicted that most pits would close if the miners lost the strike. The strike ended in 1985, and by 1992 most pits were closed. The choir sang during rallies throughout South Wales in the 1992 campaign to stop pit closures. In Newport, Reverend Rowan Williams, the present Archbishop of Canterbury, and Tyrone O'Sullivan of Tower NUM addressed a rally in John Frost Square. We sang, and a Welsh band in kilts played bagpipes.

The highlight of the Stop Pit Closure campaign was a candlelight vigil by the Nye Bevan statue in Queen Street, Cardiff at Christmas 1992. Amongst the Labour

Rhymney Miners' Support Group included Côr Cochion Caerdydd members Dave Hill, Steve Wride, Ray Davies and Colin Matthews

MPs at the vigil was Rhodri Morgan, the present First Minister of the National Assembly for Wales.

The red flag was first raised in 1831 by the workers in Wales. Tower Colliery NUM were short of ox blood when they re-enacted this historic moment on Chartist Day 13th November 1993. We stood on a hillside on Hirwaun common, brandishing an array of brightly-coloured umbrellas attempting to sing, as the rain lashed down and the wind tore at our umbrellas. The white sheet was dipped in vegetarian red dye. It emerged like the present Labour Party, a very pale pink. Undeterred, the miners carried it aloft on a flagpole as we battled against the storm down the hill to Hirwaun.

The miners of Tower NUM bought the pit and it re-opened January 2nd 1995. On a crisp winter's morning, the miners and their supporters wound their way up the bleak sunlit hillside to the pit, with bands playing, trade union banners raised high, flags flying – and we know, because we were there.

Seven years later, this pit – which the Tory government said was not economically viable – is still making a profit.

Switch on for the Miners. Queen Street, Cardiff, Christmas 1992

MINER'S LIFEGUARD

USA Miner, 1890's.
Music from 'Life's Railroad to
Heaven' by Abbey and Tillman

1. Miner's life is like a sailor's,
   'Board a ship to cross the waves.
   Every day his life's in danger,
   Still he ventures being brave.
   Watch the rocks, they're falling daily,
   Careless miners always fail;
   Keep your hand upon your wages,
   And your eyes upon the scale.
      Union miners, stand together,
      Do not heed the owners' tale.
      Keep your hand upon your wages,
      And your eyes upon the scale.

2. You've been docked and docked again, boys,
   You've been loading two for one.
   What have you to show for working,
   Since your mining days begun?
   Worn-out boots and worn-out miners,
   And the children looking pale
   Keep your hand upon your wages,
   And your eyes upon the scale.

3. In conclusion bear in memory,
   Keep this password in your mind:
   God provides for every worker
   When in union they combine.
   Men and women stand together;
   Victory for you'll prevail,
   Keep your hand upon your wages,
   And your eyes upon the scale.
      Union miners, stand together,
      Do not heed the owners' tale.
      Keep your hand upon your wages,
      And your eyes upon the scale.

Chapter Three

Women of the Working Class

What women's liberation failed to move
this strike has mobilized, 1984–1985

With the collapse of C.O.W. (Choir of Women) a group of very strong, liberated women joined Côr Cochion Caerdydd. Miners from the South Wales Valleys, with traditional male chauvinist views, were in for a shock at their first rehearsal. To them, 'socialist choir' meant 'male voice choir'. This was a mixed choir – with women. Women so different from their mothers, wives and daughters that they could have been another breed, or possibly from another planet. But the women from the valleys were changing. They were not only serving in the soup kitchens. Those who had not been interested in the Women's Liberation Movement of the 1970's became politically educated during the strike. They found their voices, spoke at meetings, and joined our choir.

Many of the women who were politicized during the miners strike 1984–85 went on to learn about the radical issues of the 1980's and 1990's. In the 21st century they are involved in organising the fight against homophobia,

Choir women (and Ray Davies) support CPSA strike, winter 1996-7. A woman's place is in her union.

International Women's Day, 8 March 2002. Choir with Violet John and mother from Holy Cross School, Belfast

racism, and globalization. They are demanding self-determination and peace with justice in Northern Ireland, Western Sahara and Palestine. The list is endless.

Here we go for the Women of the Working Class
Words and music by Mal Finch, 1984–85

Chorus:
We are women.
We are strong.
We are fighting for our lives.
Side by side with the men who work the nation's mines,
United by the struggle,
United by the past,
And it's…
Here we go, here we go for the women of the working class.

1. Don't need government approval for everything we do,
We don't need their permission to have a point of view.
Don't need anyone to tell us what to think or what to say,
We've strength enough and wisdom of our own
To go our own way.

Chorus: We are women etc.

2. They talk about statistics, about the price of coal,
The cost is the communities dying on the dole.
In fighting for our future we find ways to organise.
Where women's liberation failed to move,
This strike has mobilized.

Chorus: We are women etc

3. Ours is a unity that threats can never breach,
Ours an education that books could never teach.
We've faced the taunts and violence,
Of Maggie's thugs in blue,
When you're fighting for survival,
You've got nothing, nothing left to lose.

International Women's Day, 8 March, 2002.
Supporting Women in Palestine

WOMEN OF THE WORKING CLASS

We are women, we are strong, we are fighting for our lives, side by side with the men who work the nation's mines. U-nited by the struggle, u-nited by the past, and it's Here we go, here we go, for the women of the working class. Don't need government ap- proval for everything we do. We don't need their per- mission to have a point of view. Don't need anyone to tell us what to think or what to say. We've strength enough and wisdom of our own to go our own way

Chapter Four

Side by Side
with the People of Spain, 1986

50th to 60th Anniversaries of the 1936 Spanish Civil War and the International Brigade 1986 to 1996

International Brigade, Spanish Civil War, 1936. Unveiling the Monument in the Garden of Remembrance, Cardiff, 27 October, 1992. Left to right: unknown, Jim Brewer, Fred Thomas, Walter Greenhalgh, Maurice Levitas, Griff Jones, Bill Alexander, unknown, Alun Menai Williams, Morien Morgan, Lance Rogers

Jim Brewer of the International Brigade in Wales gave fulsome praise to the choir when we performed at an International Brigaders' rally in Abertridwr, Mid Glamorgan in the summer of 1986. He was disappointed that we didn't sing 'Bread of Heaven', which is sung to the tune 'Cwm Rhondda'. He said that 'Bread of Heaven' was sung by the Welsh contingent on the hunger marches of the 1930's. Many of the stalwarts of the hunger marches had joined the International Brigade and taken this hymn with them to Spain. The choir use the tune 'Cwm Rhondda' for the rousing song 'Buddugoliaeth Gwerin Gwlad' (victory to the working

Meeting for International Brigade, addressed by Michael Foot. Mid Glamorgan County Hall, 25 September, 1992

Monument commermorating the International Brigade, designed by Wendy Lewis. Bernard Jones is seen giving it a spring clean.

people) by Niclas y Glais.

During 1986 and the following decade, we were privileged to meet and perform for most of the survivors of the British contingent of the International Brigade. We also met the Spanish Ambassador, Michael Foot M.P., and Professor Gwyn Alf Williams.

The foremost objective of these rallies was the need to remind succeeding generations of the reason why the International Brigade fought to defend the Spanish government in the Spanish Civil War. It was a war to defend democracy and to fight fascism. The other objective of the rallies was to campaign and raise money for memorials to be erected in memory of the International Brigaders. The first to be erected in Britain was in London, while the first in Cardiff was in the Garden of Remembrance. This was followed by plaques and memorial stones throughout South Wales. Ray and Wendy represented the choir when the first memorial in Spain was unveiled on Jarama bridge.

None of the International Brigaders were present on one memorable occasion in Tonypandy. The choir remained on stage, facing the audience after the film *Land and Freedom* by Ken Loche had been shown. A heated discussion then took place between the audience of anarchists, the Trotskyists and the communists which was reminiscent of *Clochemerle*. Reviving the quarrels of the 1930's, the Anarchists said the Communists had taken all their orders from Stalin and wouldn't give non-Communists arms, while the Communists said the Anarchists would only work eight-hour shifts. As this farce unfolded, and one after another they creaked to their feet, the choir stared ahead inscrutably, not daring to look at each other.

VALLEY OF JARAMA

Words: Alex McDaid
Music: Red River Valley

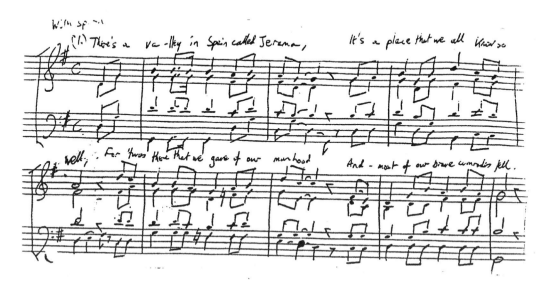

There's a valley in Spain called Jarama,
It's a place that we all know so well,
for 'twas there that we gave of our life's blood
and most of our brave comrades fell.

We are proud of the British Batallion
And the stand for Madrid that they made
With the women who fought there besides them
In the ranks of the fifteenth brigade.

With the rest of the International column
In the fight for the freedom of Spain
For they vowed at the valley of Jarama
That fascism never should reign.

We have left that dark valley forever
But the memory will always remain
of our struggle for freedom and justice
Side by side with the people of Spain.

Chapter Five

Watch Out. There's a Rumble of War

Peace is not the absence of war, 1987

"When we fight, provoked by their aggression,
Let us be inspired by life and love."
Billy Bragg, in his version of 'The Internationalé' in 1990

Côr Cochion Caerdydd is not a pacifist choir, although it has many pacifist members. It is opposed to the wars provoked by capitalist governments for economic control of world resources and to wars provoked to boost sales for the arms industries.

The earliest television footage of the choir was at a CND rally during the Miners' Strike, possibly in Chesterfield, in 1984. Arthur Scargill was one of the speakers.

By 1987, the choir was singing regularly at the CND Wales Anti-Apartheid stall, in front of Caerffili Castle. We also appeared in festivals in Newport, Gwent, demonstrations in Barry and

On the march along Queen St, Cardiff, with CND about 1988

Cardiff and fundraising events to establish the Peace Shop in Mackintosh Place, Cardiff.

Anti-War demonstration during Afghan war. Wednesday 3rd October 2001

The former chief scientific advisor to the Ministry of Defence spoke on technology. He put the case for a new generation of sophisticated weapons to be deployed against 'terrorists' and 'rogue states'. Professor Chris Norris was invited. He was asked to

Hiroshima and Nagasaki survivors plant tree of peace opposite the National Museum in Cardiff, in memory of those who died.

bring some friends. While the guests were having their pre-lecture coffee and biscuits, the choir sang peace songs. The choir then moved to the auditorium for the meeting. They chose the most conspicuous seats, far from the doors, and overlooking the audience and speaker.

"Your description has been issued to the security staff," a friend of Professor Norris informed him. "You are not to be allowed into the auditorium for the lecture." The choir was already seated.

The choir decided not to interrupt the lecture, as Professor Norris wanted to address the audience at question time. When called to speak, Professor Norris began by pointing out that the attitude of the lecturer was amoral. The scientist had talked about the technical excellence of these weapons and other military devices,

while giving no thought to the cost in human lives. The Professor then moved on to the present international crises, including the war in Afghanistan. He covered globalisation, poverty, refugees and the major reasons why disempowered people are attracted to fanatical movements. He argued that rich nations of the world caused the poverty of poor nations. He said that the USA were top of the list of terrorist states as they were responsible for putting dictators in power in Iraq, Indonesia and Chile, to name just a few. The USA are responsible for thousands being killed, injured or becoming refugees from those dictatorships.

At the end of the meeting the choir sang:

> Technological advancement
> Should be used for human gain,
> Used for peace, not mass destruction,
> We can break the nuclear chain.
> Jobs, not bombs, is our desire;
> We don't want an Afghan war,
> We want peace, not mass destruction,
> Ban the bomb for evermore.

The guests were then invited to a buffet. Security barred our way.

"This is a private function," they informed us. We showed them our tickets and asked to see the person who had invited us.

"I think you are stepping outside your brief," Professor Norris informed them. "I am a member of staff."

"I am a County Councillor," Councillor Sue Lent said. "Shall I phone the Western Mail and inform them that a world-renowned academic and a county representative have been barred from a university function?" She took out her mobile phone and began to dial a number.

"Let's come to a compromise," said the head of security. "I will let you in if you promise not to sing."

"Shall we agree that we will not sing if anyone objects?" said a choir negotiator.

His instruction was to keep us out, but finding himself between a rock and a hard place he accepted the 'compromise'.

We went in to enjoy the wine and good food, and spread our message amongst the guests.

"Have you been invited?" a Colonel Blimp asked me.

"Of course," I smiled sweetly at him. "We couldn't have come without being invited."

One or two people were genuinely interested in the ideas the choir was putting forward. A couple of army cadets told us that they were recruited at the Freshers' Fair with a promise that their university fees would be paid if they signed up.

The choir sang a few more peace songs and ended with the Welsh national anthem and the 'Internationalé'. The acoustics were wonderful.

Celebrating the commemorative and historic site of Greenham Common women's Peace Camp, 5 October 2002

WATCH OUT!

Words & music: Holly Near

Arr: Bronwyn Westacott

Chapter Six

They Took Our Homes, They Took Our Land

Anti-Apartheid, 1988

'Choir Hits False Note With The Law.'
The Guardian, 17 February, 1988.
Article by Tony Heath and Ed Vullamy

The most memorable occasion on which the voices of the Cardiff Red Choir filled the air was two years ago when it welcomed Archbishop Desmond Tutu, who was then being honoured with the freedom of that town. That was until yesterday lunchtime, however, when every member of that worthy choral institution was back in Merthyr – this time in the dock of the magistrates' court – to receive a criminal record.

The magistrates of Merthyr found the 14 members of the choir guilty of obstruction after another less happy performance in the local shopping centre just before Christmas.

Last December 12, the choir had returned to Merthyr to offer its esteemed repertoire of Welsh airs and African songs for the benefit of the local Anti-Apartheid movement, which was staging a rather up-market demonstration on the pedestrianised precinct. The music was to provide a stirring backdrop of sound to the

Wales Anti-Apartheid Concert with Peggy Seeger, Dafydd Iwan, Dave Burns and Côr Cochion Caerdydd, at St David's Hall, Cardiff, 26 April, 1990

St. David's Hall

Thursday 26 April   7.30 p.m.

WALES ANTI-APARTHEID FREEDOM CONCERT

PEGGY SEEGER

in Concert with COR COCHION CAERDYDD
DAVE BURNS · DAFYDD IWAN
(In memory of Ewan MacColl)

£6.00 All Seats YouthCard, Children, Students, Senior Citizens, UB40s £4.00

distribution of leaflets urging shoppers to boycott South African goods.

The was no Nobel prize-winning bishop along for this event, and there was certainly no 1,000 strong crowd to admire the performance. There was, however, a Mr Paul Murray, manager of the Tesco supermarket, who beheld the ranks of singers strewn across his township and telephoned the police to complain.

"The singing was very nice," he admitted in court yesterday. "One of my staff thought it was carol singing and put 50p in the bucket."

There was an Inspector Royston Whitney, who told the court that when he arrived on the scene, he thought the choir was singing protest songs.

May Day 1993, raising awareness about apartheid

With him was P.P. Nigel Heggey, who recalled to the court, like a true son of the land of song, that 'the singing was very melodious'. He added: 'I didn't recognise the language, but I assumed they were protest songs as I'd heard something similar on television.' The choir was arrested.

The dramatis personae of the precinct protest saga was treated to a repeat performance on the steps of the magistrates' court yesterday before yesterday's hearing, but the bench were unimpressed, and decided to convict, dealing out 12 absolute discharges and two conditional discharges.

The choir's conductor, Mr John Abraham, invoked the cause of Merthyr's distinguished Freeman, arguing that Bishop Tutu would 'No doubt... have supported our action.'

Former Archbishop Desmond Tutu of South Africa greets the choir when he is awarded an Honorary Doctorate from the University of Wales, 18 April 1998.

Letter from former Archbishop Desmond Tutu, praising the choir's singing and thanking them for their commitment to anti-apartheid

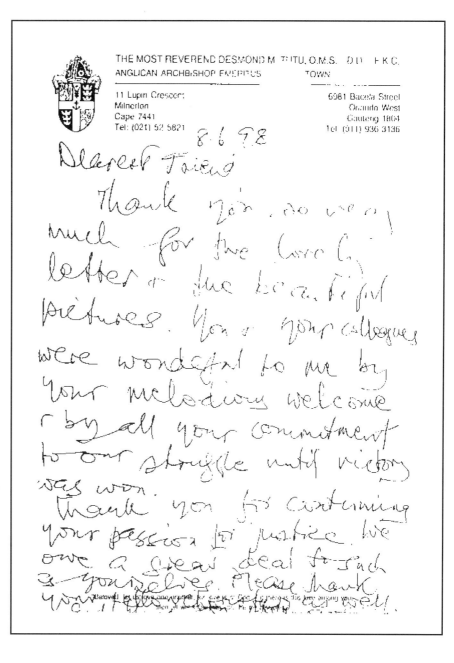

ASIKATALI/ Children of Africa

WE ARE THE CHILDREN OF AFRICA, AND ITS FOR FREEDOM THAT WE'RE FIGHTING NOW
WE DO NOT CARE IF WE GO TO PRISON, IT IS FOR FREEDOM THAT WE GLADLY GO
THEY TOOK OUR HOMES, THEY TOOK OUR LAND - HOW MUCH LONGER WILL THEY BLEED US?
IN SOWETO THEY SHOT US DOWN - BUT WE SHALL RISE UP UNITED

Chapter Seven

Adelante – Forward

Nicaraguan Revolution, 1979–1989
We are Struggling Against the Yankees – Luchamos Contra el Yanqui

When President Daniel Ortega of Nicaragua visited Britain on 8th May 1989 over 3,000 packed into Central Hall, Westminster, to hear him. The audience clapped for half an hour when he came on stage. Amongst those on stage to welcome him were Graham Green and Bianca Jagger. Schoolchildren from Mountain Ash, Mid Glamorgan presented him with a gift and letters from their classmates. Côr Cochion Caerdydd were privileged to sing the Sandinista anthem, 'Adelante'.

Before the event we had a sound check in the hall, then went to a local pub for a drink. We came out to find Young Tory supporters of the Nicaraguan Contras standing on a rostrum in the square overlooking the main door. They were shouting abuse at the queue waiting to go into the hall. Radical paper sellers started shouting back at them and the situation began to look ugly. The police, who had been observing the Contra Supporters, had done nothing to protect the people in the queue. They now began to mobilize.

Contra supporters shouting at people going into Central Hall, Westminster, for Nicaragua Solidarity rally, 8 May, 1989

The choir faced the Contra supporters and sang 'Stand up and Sing'. The Young Conservatives had never met a singing picket before and were completely thrown. The shouting faltered then ceased. The police, who had been moving in a pincer movement toward the queue, stopped.

When the song ended, the Contra supporters tried to regroup. We sang 'Adelante'. When we finished they made a feeble attempt to start shouting again.

Helen Mary Jones said, 'Let's sing 'Mandela'. That will finish their demonstration.' She was right. By the end of 'Mandela', the Contra supporters had drifted away and the police could find no excuse for arresting Nicaragua Solidarity Supporters.

When we went on stage in Central Hall to sing 'Adelante' the atmosphere was electric. The audience cheered stamped and whistled. Most of them had never heard of us before that event. We attributed this amazing welcome to our singing defeat of the Contra Supporters outside the hall.

Supporters of Sandanistas shouting at Contra supporters, Central Hall, Westminster, 8 May, 1989

ADELANTE (Sandanista hymn)
Words and music: Carlos Mejie Godoy

Adelante marchemos, compañeros,
 avancemos a la revolución!
Nuestro pueblo es el dueño de su historia
 arcitecto de su liberación.
Combatientes del Frente Sandinista,
 adelante que es nuestro porvenir!
Rojo-y-negra bandera nos cobija,
 Patria libre, vencer o morir!

Los hijos de Sandino,
 ni se venden, ni se rinden,
luchamos contra el yanqui
 enemigo del humanidad.

Adelante etc

Hoy, el amanecer
 dejó de ser una tentación.
Mañana algun día surgirá un nuevo sol,
 que va illuminar todo la tierra,
que nos llegaron los martires y heroes,
 con caudalosos rios de leche y miel.

Adelante etc.

*Côr Cochion Caerdydd and Nicaraguan President Daniel Ortega
sing 'Adelante', the hymn of the Sandanista revolution, 8 May,
1989*

ADELANTE (Sandanista hymn)
Words and music by Carlos Mejie Godoy

① Ade - lante, marchemos compañeros, Avancemos a la revolución! Nuestro
② Combatientes del frente Sandinista, Adelante quees nuestro porvenir!
Rojo—y

① pueblo es el dueño de su historia, Arquitecto de su liberación.
② negra bandera nos co—
②-bija, Patria

libre vencer o morir!
③ Los hijos de Sandino, ni se venden, ni se rinden,
Luchamos

Ah—
④ Adelante
⑤ Hoy el amanecer

contra el Yanqui, Enemigo de la humanidad.

⑤ Hoy el amanecer dejó de ser una tentación. Ma-

-ñana algun día surgirá un nuevo sol, que va' iluminar toda la

tierra, que nos llegaron los martires y heroes con caudalosos

rios de leche y miel.

recap chorus ① Adelante

Chapter Eight

Lords and Masters in their Mansions

Anti-Poll Tax Campaign, 1990
New Worker
Santa Arrested at Bargoed Magistrates' Court

The local anti-poll tax group had invited the public to a party at the court on 13th December during the hearing of poll tax cases. A Labour Councillor slipped into the court, his red cloak concealed under his anorak, while police were busy barring Mother Christmas who had arrived with a trolley-load of party goodies. Donning his outfit, he sat in the centre of the public gallery. Non-payers, many of them the poorest in the community and frightened of the court, relaxed to enjoy the entertainment. Police dragged him off to the police cells under a barrage of photographers.

Meanwhile, Mother Christmas secreted the goodies, including reindeer's antlers, about her person and in the bags of various respectable-looking friends. Once in court, she re-emerged from her anorak as a butterfly from a chrysalis, and with her two reindeer, began passing balloons, party poppers and carol singing sheets along the rows of the public gallery. The police seemed oblivious.

Mother Christmas inflated a balloon. Pandemonium broke out, party poppers banged, sending out streamers

Poll Tax Demonstration, the Mall, London, 31 March, 1990

across the court. Inflated balloons were released and coloured buntings hung around.

There was a cry of, 'Get that woman out!' but she sat on the floor, linking hands with and surrounded by confused but amused non-payers. The magistrate gave up and moved to another room.

The rest of the story involved a Christmas tree, mince pies, the Red Choir giving a carol concert and anti-Tory poems.

Wendy Lewis and Lyn Mererid dressed as reindeer, Bargoed Magistrates' Court, Thursday 13 December, 1990

This poster was fly-posted from Caerffili to Rhymney, advertising the hearings at Bargoed Magistrates Court, 13 December, 1990

LORDS AND LADIES IN THEIR MANSIONS

Words: Helen Mary Jones, Wendy Lewis, Beaty Smith
Music: Charles C Converse, 1868

① Lords and bishops in your manors, yuppies with Marina views,

city gents in country villas, Thatcher's poll tax is good news.

But for those with grown up children, when the bailiffs come to call,

'Can't pay won't pay' makes no difference, when they take away your all.

) Lords and Bishops in your manors,
Yuppies with marina views,
City Gents in country villas,
Thatcher's poll tax is good news.
But for those with grown up children,
When the bailiffs come to call,
"Can't pay won't pay" makes no difference,
When they take away your all

) Joy to those who live in cloisters,
Joy to prisoners in their cell,
Homeless people on park benches,
Thatchers poll tax treats you well.
But for those who struggle daily,
Coping but about to crack,
If you care about your family,
Dump the poll tax off your back.

. Up above the Scottish Border,
There's a million who won't pay.
While a friendly little virus
Screws the records up each day.
People's power cannot be beaten,
If we stand together strong.
Prove before the next election
A million voters can't be wrong.

Mister Major, just remember
When the tax last went ahead,
How the peasants forced surrender
And the Chancellor lost his head.
Therefore, people stand united,
As Wat Tyler did before,
Unjust laws must be resisted:
Throw the polltax out the door.

Chapter Nine

We Don't Want a Desert War

Anti-Gulf War, 1990
New Worker, 8 February, 1991

The Cardiff Reds Choir has done it again. Last month we reported their courtroom poll tax Christmas party; now their latest target is the Royal Air Force.

The RAF's high-powered and over-funded public relations team planned a film and talk aimed at top academics and other bigwigs. But one of the university's academics is also a member the Reds Choir and got tickets for his singing friends, and they infiltrated the meeting disguised as ordinary people. After the film, as the RAF group captain rose to speak, so did a member of the Red Choir. He addressed the meeting, expressing concern for, 'our boys in the Gulf'. Most people thought it was all part of the show. He went on to demand the 'boys' be brought home – because they shouldn't have been sent there in the first place. Then the whole choir assembled and sang anti-war songs for half an hour. The audience loved the J.S. Bach arrangement of 'The Whole Wide World Around' and gave us an enthusiastic round of applause. It was only when the university security tried to evict us that it gradually dawned on the academics that we were not part of the programme.

We had just finished singing 'Mae Hen Wlad Fy Nhadau' (the Welsh national anthem) and started the 'Internationalé' when the police arrived. A choir spokesperson told the police we would be leaving after this song.

We don't want a desert war.
Houses of Parliament, London, September 1990

"That's fine," said the officer. "Why aren't you on your usual spot by the market?"

"We were invited to this meeting, see, so we could turn down the invitation."

We danced down the stairs and out of the building, singing:

I'm gonna lay down my sword and shield
Down by the riverside.

Candlelight vigil against the Gulf War, January 1991, Queen Street, Cardiff, south Wales

JOBS NOT BOMBS.   Words by Dave Hill

1. Stop and think about your neighbour,
   If you want all threats to cease.
   Don't forget that they   must labour.
   And deserve to live in peace.

chorus

   Jobs not bombs is our desire,
   We don't want a nuclear war,
   We want peace not mass destruction,
   Ban the bomb for ever more.

2. There's a fact thats quite apparent,
   Well beknown to you and I,
   No such thing as a deterrent,
   It's a lousy wicked lie.
   (chorus)

3. Greenham Common cruise is haunting,
   In defiance of our will,
   Hopes of peace it's daily taunting,
   With its awful threat to kill:
   (chorus)

4. Technological advancement,
   Should be used for human gain,
   Used for peace, not mass destruction,
   We can break the nuclear chain.

Singing for sanctions against Iraq to be lifted. Abergavenny, 2000

JOBS NOT BOMBS

Music: John Hughes, Glan-dŵr, Abertawe

Chapter Ten

Only Our Rivers Run Free

Derry, Ireland, 1992. 20th Anniversary of Bloody Sunday

The people gathered silently
To march to Guildhall Square;
They came in peace to state their case
Among their own kind there.
But butchers waited there for them
With bullet, blood and pain,
And fourteen men will never walk
On Derry streets again.

'Côr Cochion Caerdydd (The Cardiff Reds Choir) were next and it would probably be fair to say that they stole the show. Their set included a song that had been written specially for the commemoration about Bloody Sunday entitled 'Derry Streets', which they sang to the air of 'The Foggy Dew', and merited the first of two standing ovations the group were to receive. Although they call themselves a choir, they don't exactly sing hymns and arias. They are more of a campaigning outfit, with song topics ranging from the killing of whales to Nelson Mandela. Johnny Walker, who was in the audience, was persuaded to join the group to accept a cheque for £450 the choir had raised in Cardiff for the BSI and as Mr Walker was leaving the stage, he was presented with a portrait of himself by Tony Doherty,

Guildhall Square, Derry. 20th Anniversary of Bloody Sunday, 25 January, 1992

Garvaghy Road, Drumcree, 6 July, 1997. Roman Catholics held mass surrounded by British tanks. The choir led the singing. The people were not allowed to go to church

Garvaghy Road, Drumcree, Northern Ireland, 5 July 1997. Wendy making a banner.

BSI. The choir also invited relatives of Bloody Sunday victims to appear with them and ended off their set with the 'Internationalé' sung in Welsh and the (Irish) national anthem, in Gaelige, if you don't mind.'
Derry Journal, Tuesday 28th January, 1992

The choir first visited Northern Ireland in August 1990, as part of the British Troops Out Movement Delegation. In July 1997 we were privileged to be invited by the Garvaghy Road residents in Drumcrie who were trying to stop the Orange Lodge marching through their estate. We visited the Women's Peace camp before and after it was destroyed by the RUC. We brought greetings from Wales CND. Residents sitting on the road told us that our part was to sing and observe. Afterwards protestors thanked us. They felt isolated until we sang. As women demonstrators were thrown from the road over a barrier of armoured cars by the RUC we stood on a wall, facing the army and RUC, singing:

We shall overcome,
We shall overcome,
We shall overcome some day.
We are not afraid,
We are not afraid.

An Irishman called up as he ran past, 'Well, I bloody am!'

When the Catholic community was prevented from going to mass by the RUC and Army, the choir led the singing for the mass held on the village green.

Only Our Rivers Run Free
Arranged by John Abraham of Côr Cochion Caerdydd, and the Wolfe Tones.

When apples still grow in November,
When blossoms still grow from each tree,
When leaves are still green in December,
It's then that our land will be free.
I wander her hills and her valleys
But still, through my sorrow, I see
A land that has never known freedom,
And only her rivers run free.

I drink to the death of her people,
To those who would rather have died
Than to live in the cold chains of bondage.
To bring back their rights was denied.
Oh where are you now that we need you?
What burns where the flames used to be?
Are you gone like the snows of last winter
And will only our rivers run free.

How sweet is life, but we're crying.
How mellow the wine, but we're dry.
How fragrant the rose but it's dying.
How gentle the breeze, but it sighs.
What good is in youth when it's ageing?
What joy is in eyes that cant see?
When there's sorrow in sunshine and flowers
And still only our rivers run free.

ONLY OUR RIVERS RUN FREE

arr Wolfe Tones/John

Words and music: Michael MacConnell

When apples still grow in No·vember, when blossoms still grow from each

tree, when leaves are still green in De·cember, it's then that our

land will be free. I wander her hills and her valleys, _ but

still through my sorrow I see, a land that has never known

freedom, and only her rivers run free.

Chapter Eleven

You can't stop here.
Get along – move! Go! Shift!

1993, Asylum Seekers

When a Welsh choir from Cardiff offered to sing for asylum seekers in Campsfield detention centre, Oxford at Christmas 2000, we were a slightly welcome diversion from the tedious life there. Bored residents waited in the half-empty church-cum-meeting hall. Shocking them out of their complacency with 'Ha Ji Ah Mozambique', we then moved on through our Palestinian and South African repertoire. The air was electric as they stamped, clapped, sang and danced along with us. During the refreshment break they told their friends about the concert. The second half of the concert was standing or dancing room only. The hall resounded with singing from the audience while the guards stood by looking bemused.

The Oxford asylum seekers support group climb barriers and struggled through undergrowth every month to shout messages of support over the thirty foot double fence around the exercise yard. The choir joined them every six months since 1994. Until 2000 we had never been inside. We hoped to make these concerts a regular event, but despite our best efforts we have never been invited back. The residents are not there to enjoy themselves. We are back where we belong, singing outside the fence.

Campsfield Detention Centre, Oxford. Singing to asylum seekers through thirty-foot double fences, August 1998

Moving On Song
Words and music by Ewan McColl
Arranged by Wendy Lewis

Born in the middle of the afternoon
In a horse-drawn waggon on the old A5.
The big twelve-wheeler shook my bed.
"You can't stop here," the policeman said

Chorus:
So you'd better get born in someplace else
So move along, get along,
Move along, get along, go! Move! Shift!

Born in the tattie-lifting time,
In an old bell tent in a tattie field days,
The farmer said, 'The work's all done.
It's time that you were moving on…'

Chorus

Born on the common, near a building site,
Where the ground was rutted by the trailers' wheels.
The local people said to me,
'You'll lower the price of property'.

Chorus

Wagon tent or trailer born,
Last month, last year or in far off days,
Born here or a thousand miles away,
There's always those nearby who'll say

Chorus

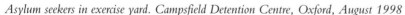
Asylum seekers in exercise yard. Campsfield Detention Centre, Oxford, August 1998

Raising awareness about the rights of asylum seekers.
The Hayes, Cardiff, 2001

MOVING ON (TRAVELLER'S SONG)

Ewan McColl/WAL

born in the middle of the af-ter-noon in a horse drawn wagon on the old A — five the big twelve wheeler shook my bed "You can't stop here" the policeman said, so you better get born in some place else so move a-long get a-long move along get a-long go! move! shift!

Chapter Twelve

Our Roots are in the Soil
Choir Tour, Palestine and Israel, 1994

'We are like an olive tree. Our roots are in the soil.
No matter what tragedies befall us,
we shall remain on our land.'

Thursday 21st, April 1994, the choir spent the day in Gaza. Palestinian children at the YWCA school sang to us and we sang to them.

A meeting for women, in the main hall, was being addressed by a European man. We were not officially singing, but once again, we found ourselves on stage giving a concert. 'Women of the Working Class' from the 1984/5 miners strike was greeted with a standing ovation. This may appear to be a male-dominated society, but the women are very strong. Ignoring the lecture on health to which they had just been subjected, the meeting was followed by calorie-rampant trays of sticky cakes and sugary drinks. There is 80% unemployment in Gaza, but everywhere we went that day the people pressed food and drink on us.

In Jabalia refugee camp we visited the only medical facilities for the 70,000 refugees. It consisted of a gynaecology examination room, a dental surgery and a general purpose treatment room.

Launch of Palestine Cassette. House of Commons, London.

We asked a group of children could we take their photographs. They agreed, then one of the boys stepped away from the group.

"I'm an Israeli soldier," he said to the others. "Where is your identity pass?" And he walked along the row, slapping them across their heads.

We met the parents of the first boy to die in the intifada (uprising) of 1987. Next we met a wheelchair-bound survivor.

The world and her husband were on the sand or in the water when we went down to the Mediterranean beach. The young men were on home-made surfboards while the girls had to be satisfied with paddling in saturated long dresses.

The choir conductor and deputy conductor were Jewish. For our return journey through Israel by coach, they sat on the front two seats. We put away our Palestinian scarves and flags and transformed ourselves into European tourists, with flamboyant sun hats, baseball caps and large flashy cameras. At the checkpoint the soldiers boarded the coach carrying their rifles. We were reminded of a similar experience in Northern Ireland. We waved our British passports and were as loud, friendly, and cheerful as possible. After we had been allowed to drive off the driver discovered we were carrying four students back to Birzeit University. He was furious with us. He could have lost his job. The worst that could have happened to us was deportation.

A few days later, the university was raided by the Israeli army during the night. Many escaped into the surrounding hills, but those caught without the necessary papers were deported back to Gaza.

Children in Palestine, Choir Tour, April, 1994

Mayday, Nazareth. Choir Tour of Palestine, Israel, 1994

MOWTINI – MY HOMELAND

MOWTINEE   MOWTINEE
AL-JA -MA-LOO WAL-JA- LA -LOO
WAL- HA- YA- TOO WAL-NA- JA- TOO
FEE ROO-BAK   FEE ROO-BAK
WAL- HA- NA-O , WAL-RA-JA-O
WAL-SA-NA-O,   WAL-HA-WA-O,
FEE HAWAK,   FEE HA-WAK
HUL A-RAK,   HUL A-RAK
SAL-EE-MAN - MOO-NA-A-MAN, WA-RA-NEE-MAN, MOO--KAR-A -MAN,
SAL-EE-MAN - MOO-NA-A-MAN, WA-RA-NEE-MAN, MOO--KAR-A -MAN,
HUL A-RAK,   FEE OW-LAK,
TAB-LOO-ROO-SEE-MA, TAB-LOO-ROO-SEE-MA,
MOWTINEE   MOWTINEE

MOWTINEE,   MOWTINEE
AL-SHE-BAR-BOO, LEN-YE-KIL-LE
AS-MOO-HOO, EN-YES-TE-KIL-LE,
O YE-BEED   O YE-BEED,
NES-TE-KEE- MIN-E-RA-DA
WEL-LEN-NA-KOO-NA LI-LAY-DA
KEL A-BEED   KEL A-BEED
LAN-O-REED,   LAN-O-REED,
AY-SHEN-AL-MOO-NEK-A-DA, WE-THIL-LAN AL-MO -AY -BED-DA
AY-SHEN-AL-MOO-NEK-A-DA, WE-THIL-LAN AL-MO -AY -BED-DA
LAN-O-REED,   BEL-NA-EED,
MEJ-DEN E-TEL-EED. MEJ-DEN E-TEL-EED.

Chapter Thirteen

Change will not come from above
Liverpool Dockers 1995–1998

The annual Christmas pub crawl 1995 was in aid of the children of the striking Liverpool dockers. The choir sang well-known carols such as 'Nkosi Sikalali'.

We sang every Tuesday throughout the three-year strike. Benefits were held in pubs. We also picketed the heliport and docks in Cardiff. In the first two months to

Supporting Liverpool Dockers on the Hayes,
28 September 1995 – 26 January 1998

Christmas 1995 we had raised £1,600. The following Christmas, 1996, a choir member was on the picket line in Liverpool at 6 a.m. and handed over a cheque from the choir.

One freezing morning at 5 a.m. we formed a singing picket at the dock gates in Cardiff, stopping the traffic to protest against goods being diverted from Liverpool. The management came to negotiate with us while they waited for the police to arrive to remove us. Meanwhile a Cardiff docker had been leading two Liverpool dockers onto the docks by an unguarded path. Our diversion tactics worked. The Liverpool dockers were able to climb the gantry undisturbed, stop any further unloading, and get their picture in the South Wales Echo to publicise their cause.

Meanwhile, having played our part we were desperate to find a women's toilet or a tree. Both being rather scarce in the empty streets of Butetown at 5.30 a.m. we took turns to crouch over a street drain.

This picket was the legendary occasion when one chorister sang, 'all hateful enemies go for a walk', when she meant, 'all hateful enemies are put to flight'. She sang, 'pob gelyn cas yn mynd am dro' instead of 'pob gelyn cas yn mynd ar ffo'.

At the end of the strike, the choir was presented with a certificate signed by Tony Russell, Merseyside Port shop steward.

"Who speaks of defeat? I tell you, a cause like ours is greater than defeat can know it. It is the power of powers." – James Larkin.

LIVERPOOL DOCKERS
Support Group South Wales

This certificate of thanks is in recognition of the socialist solidarity and

the consistent commitment to raising much needed

finance shown by the Red Choir

from the Liverpool Dockers and your comrades in the Support Group.

You can be proud to have played a part in the great dispute of the 500 Sacked Liverpool Dock Workers 28 September 1995 - 26 January 1998 which marks the resurgence of the best traditions of trade unionism and class struggle in this country and internationally.

"Who is it speaks of defeat? I tell you a cause like ours is greater than defeat can know it. It is the power of powers." --- James Larkin

Mariam Kamish, South Wales
Support Group Secretary

Tony Russell, Merseyside Port
Shop Steward

Liverpool Dockers' Support Group, South Wales, present the choir with a certificate. The strike lasted from September 1995 to January 1998

Liverpool Dockers' Strike. 'You are now entering Liverpool Scab Port'. At 6 a.m., Christmas 1996, a cheque from the choir was donated to the pickets

BILLY BRAGG'S INTERNATIONALE

Words: Billy Bragg
Tune: after Degeyter

Arr: David Bedford /
John Abraham

Verse 2:
Let no-one build walls to divide us,
Walls of hatred, nor walls of stone;
Oh greet the dawn and come and join us
We'll live together or we'll die alone.
In our world, poisoned by exploitation,
those who have taken, now they must give
And end the vanity of nations,
We've but one earth on which to live. (Chorus)

Verse 3:
And so begins the final drama
In the streets and in the fields
We'll stand unbowed before their armour
We defy their guns and shields.
When we fight, provoked by their aggression
Let us be inspired by life and love,
For though they offer us concessions,
Change will not come from above. (Chorus)

Chapter Fourteen

With the Poor of the Earth
Cuba Solidarity 1996.
Guantanamera. Con los pobres de la tierra

At dawn, one dull April morning in 1996 we sang the Welsh national anthem, and the 'Internationalé' as Lo Entropy sailed out of Bristol docks bound for Cuba with a cargo of aid from all over Britain. It was going to play its part in breaking the trade embargo imposed by the USA. The Lo Entropy project was the brainchild of Geofrey Böene who had gone AWOL from the Apartheid South African army and joined Wales Anti-Apartheid and the choir when he arrived as an exile in Wales. Geof saw the USA as the big bully attacking the little fellow and was convinced he had to give practical support to Cuba.

Cymru Ciwba (Cuba Solidarity Wales) was founded in 1982. They are campaigning for an end to the blockade imposed on Cuba by the USA, and also provide educational and medical aid. Cymru Ciwba was among the first organisations on the choir programme. We made enjoyable visits to Theatre Clwyd, usually in the winter, arriving to sing in the afternoon. After bedding down in sleeping bags in a historic timbered house overnight we had delightful journeys through the snow- covered mountains and woodland of North Wales.

Over the years a number of choir members have gone on solidarity tours or work delegations to Cuba, visiting schools, hospitals and mines or helping with the sugar harvest. We have been hosted by Cubans in their

Cymru Cuba Solidarity, Theatr Clwyd, North Wales 1988

End the Illegal Blockade of Cuba. European Parliament. Brussels

from Cuba. During the strike of tugboat men in 1993 we took a young Cuban delegate to Cardiff Docks to meet the men on the picket line. The strikers knew the choir as we had been supporting them. The tugboat men were being treated badly by the media and it opened their eyes. They realised they could have been misinformed about Cuba. Because of this they gave the Cuban a sympathetic hearing and presented him with a painting of the waterfront.

Every summer, the choir sings at a ceremony which is held outside the civic buildings in Cardiff when a container of educational aid – from simple requirements like pens and paper to computers – and medical aid – from cotton wool to hospital beds – is sent to Cuba from Wales.

homes, given parties by community committees from their meagre rations, met infants dancing in playgrounds, and pregnant mums in clinics. We met the committee running El Cobre copper mine. It had men and women members in equal numbers. We were fed in the works canteen, along with the pregnant mums from the village of El Cobre. They were given lunch there every day to ensure they are well-nourished. All over Cuba pregnant women go to their local factory to eat. At the end of the visit to the mine we were given a model of the Virgin of El Cobre to present to Tower Colliery, South Wales NUM. El Cobre had received safety boots and helmets from Tower Colliery NUM.

The choir has sung in the presence of Mari Florez, the Cuban Ambassador, on a number of occasions. We also have visitors

Cymru Cuba, 1988. Campaigning on the Hayes, Cardiff

CYMORTH MEDDYGOL I GIWBA

CUBA–CYMRU supports the CUBAN PEOPLE suffering under the ILLEGAL U.S. BLOCKADE Devastated by HURRICANE

GUANTANAMERA

Words: Jose Marti

Mi verso es de un verde claro
Y de un carmin encendido
Mi verso es de un verde claro
Y de un carmin encendido
Mi verso es un ciervo herido
Que busca en el monte amparo

Con los pobres de la tierra
Quiero yo mi suerte echar
Con los pobres de la tierra
Quiero yo mi suerte echar
El arroyo de la sierra
Me complace mas que el mar.

Chapter Fifteen

Yes for Wales

National Assembly for Wales, 18 September 1997

"Good morning, and it is a very good morning," announced Ron Davies, Secretary of State for Wales, on Friday 19th September, 1997. The crowd outside the old City Hall in Cardiff cheered until they were hoarse. The campaign for the National Assembly for Wales had been won by a hair's breadth. For the Assembly: 559,419; against the Assembly: 552,698.

Received history remembers the Carmarthenshire result, but Cardiff should be remembered as the result that swayed the vote in favour of an assembly. The choir worked tirelessly on the streets of Cardiff from the beginning of the campaign. At first we were met with a negative response, but we didn't let it get us down. As referendum day drew nearer we redoubled our efforts. We sang 'Yes for Wales' on the *BBC Today* programme and for American TV . Every day we could be seen singing and talking to the public in Cardiff city centre, in suburban main streets or

Yes for Wales 1997, Welsh Assembly referendum campaign, Caerffili, August 1997

MEMBERS OF Cymdeithas yr Iaith Gymraeg during their candlelight vigil on the steps of the Welsh Office in Cathays Park, Cardiff, last night.

Language society braves weather for all-night vigil

By CLIVE BETTS

REVOLUTIONARY songs wafted across Cathays Park last night as members of Côr Cochion Caerdydd joined the first part of an all-night language vigil outside the Welsh Office.

The Cardiff Red Choir, well-known at protests in the city, were supporting members of Cymdeithas yr Iaith Gymraeg who were pledged to brave the wind and cold until 9am this morning.

Later during the night, the protesters were due to be joined by actor Dewi Pws and pop singer Cedwyn Aled.

At the vigil's end, the language society members were to accompany to Cardiff magistrates' court three leading members charged with criminal damage — painting Deddf Iaith Newydd (A New Language Act) on the walls of the Welsh Office earlier this year.

The three are Dafydd Iwan, of Caernarfon, vice-president of Plaid Cymru, Dr Dyfed Elis Gruffudd, an official of the National Museum of Wales, Drefach Felindre, and Me Parri, of Taliesin, near A ystwyth, who works at the Ce for Alternative Technology, Corris.

Earlier yesterday, a d society members invaded Hayes Post Office in the ce of Cardiff and ripped up all English-language pamph they could find.

Mr Alun Llwyd, chairman the society's status group an leader of the demonstration, s "We found a large number leaflets in English, but only in Welsh, which dealt Christmas. We left that lea untouched."

In their place, the society posters with the words "Bra Swyddfa Post" (Treachery of Post Office) printed over a c of the Post Office's 1975 langu policy. Mr Llwyd said, "Ther a big difference between w they said they would do and w they have achieved."

The choir supports an all-night vigil by Cymdeithas yr Iaith Gymraeg (the Welsh Language Society), 7 December, 1988

in Splott indoor market. In the evenings we were telephone canvassing. We sang from Pontypridd to Cardiff on the Freedom march that had started from the National Eisteddfod in Bala. Cardiff voted 'no', but what

a 'no'! At the beginning of the campaign, nobody could have expected almost 50,000 people in Cardiff to vote for a National Assembly for Wales. Those in Cardiff who voted for the Assembly might not have been affected

Census 2001. We demand a 'Nationality' box for the Welsh. Welsh Office, November 2000

in hard chairs smoking and drinking wine. At 3.50 a.m. Carmarthenshire clinched it for the Assembly.

The celebration party was at the Park Hotel. There were 400 in the hall, and the choir outside. Nobody had offered us tickets. Once again we were fortunate. MEP Eluned Morgan is an ex-choir member. She told security they had to let us in as we had done all the work to make this celebration possible. And so we sang, shouted and cheered until dawn, particularly when the leaders of the political parties arrived and joined hands on the platform. At first light on a drizzling autumn morning, we dance along Queen Street in a state of euphoria, then home to bed. Some didn't bother sleeping and went to the old City Hall to hear Ron Davies wish them a very good morning.

On Saturday the choir was invited to sing at celebrations all over town. We started at the United Nations Association in the Temple of Peace, then we sang in our usual spot on the Hayes in Cardiff city centre. Cardiff West Plaid Cymru (Party of Wales) feted us next, and our host was puzzled when we included Palestinian songs in our programme. He is secretary of a Pro-Israeli group. It hasn't clouded his judgement of the choir. He

by the efforts of the choir, but we are glad that we played our part.

Foot soldiers were locked out of the action at the College of Music and Drama, where the VIPs were having an orgy of self-congratulation as the results came in, while we were singing in the rain. Fortunately one of the choir members, Sue Lent, is a councillor. She rescued us and took us into the beautiful old City Hall. After a spectacular result in Rhondda at 3 a.m. it was nail-biting swings and roundabouts. Dishevelled and apprehensive, we watched the TV screen as we slouched recently wrote a half-page article about the choir in an American magazine for expatriate Welsh people.

Our next performance was for the Communist Party of Britain, who laid on a lavish buffet.

The last event of the evening was a party at the home of Diana Bianchi, one of the founder members of the choir. We needed a Union Jack, as we knew she would want to burn one. The little spare time we had on Saturday afternoon was spent visiting flag shops and asking whether they had a Union Jack. None of them had, and looked at us rather strangely, as the only people they associate with the Union Jack are the British National Party. One of the choir suggested we asked for a box of England's Glory matches at the same time. Finally we called at a tourist shop opposite Cardiff Castle. Looking very embarrassed, and making sure no other customers were looking, he took out a parcel wrapped in brown paper from under the counter. It was an inflammable cotton Union Jack, but at £39 we decided it wasn't exactly what we were looking for. We bought a sheet of paper and coloured pens and Lyn painted the Union Jack. It burned lovely.

All The Tories Failed in Wales
(General Election 2001)
Words: Plaid Cymru Councillors Phil Bevan, John Taylor and Lindsay Whittle
Music: John Hughes, Llantwit

Felix Aubel
Maureen Kelly Owen
David Simmons
Bronwen Naish
Ian Oakley
Margaret Harper
Prudence Daily
Simon Hayes

Chorus;
Failed in Wales (3 repeats)
All the Tories Failed in Wales
(Basses – once again)
All The Tories Failed in Wales

Nigel Evans
Leader of Welsh Tories
Had to find an English seat
Throughout Wales
The same old story
One and all, they face defeat.

Chorus;
Failed in Wales (etc)

ALL THE TORIES FAILED IN WALES

Chapter Sixteen

Goodbye Gap, Goodbye Shell, Goodbye Coca Cola, 1998

Anti-globalization, Cancel Third World Debt, Alternative Summit, Save the Planet, Cardiff, 1998

We wanted a television or radio personality to promote the World Development Movement campaign against tobacco marketing in the 3rd world in 1998. The best place for meeting celebrities in Wales is at the National Eisteddfod in August. At any other time of the year they are bound to go past if you hang around the Hayes in Cardiff city centre. Boyd Clack, star of *Satellite City*, was a regular contributor to the causes we espoused. It was his lucky day when he stopped for a cup of tea at the Hayes Island Snack Bar. Two weeks later he was posing for the South Wales Echo beside a mammoth ice cream cornet, decorated with a cigarette in place of a chocolate flake. Tobacco barons in South America had been giving away cigarettes with ice cream. Another ploy to get teenagers smoking was to put on a dance and give away free cigarettes as the youngsters came in.

'Remember Tryweryn' appeared on our placards during the 1999–2002 campaign to stop the Turkish government building the Ilisu dam and drowning Kurdish villages, orchards and farms. The people of Wales immediately identified with the campaign.

Despite protests in the 1950s from all Welsh Members of Parliament, the local council, and

Shell poisons land, sea and air. Picket of Shell garage, to protest against Nigerian state murder of Ken Saro-Wiwa

outcry and demonstrations in Wales and Liverpool, the people of Tryweryn, near Bala in North Wales, were moved forty years ago, and their village, graveyard and farmlands were drowned under the reservoir named Llyn Celyn.

Ray Davies, a choir member, raised the matter of the Ilisu Dam in Caerfilli County Council. It was not strictly a local council matter, but he raised it by arguing that with the present water shortage in Britain, it was possible that a village in a valley in Caerffili might be drowned by the British Government.

27th January, 2001 was the fortieth anniversary of the closure of Tryweryn railway station. On a bright winter's morning, the choir were amongst people from all parts of Wales gathered by Llyn Celyn. A Kurdish dance group managed not only to keep their feet, but to perform intricate dance routines on the muddy bank beside the lake.

In 2002, Balfour Beatty withdrew financial support from the Ilisu Dam. Other dams are still being built in Kurdistan.

Boyd Clack supporting 1998 campaign against tobacco barons

Banana workers fighting for trade union rights, October 1997

The drowning of Kurdish homes by the Ilisu Dam and the drowning of Tryweryn by Celyn lake were linked on the 40th Anniversary of Tryweryn, 27 January, 01

CO-OPERATION REIGNS

Words: Paul Spencer, 2000

Traditional Irish Tune: "I'm Leaving Tipperary"

Arranged: Miguel Heatwole, 2000

Soprano: Although we live beneath the cloud of greedy cor-por - a - tions we must believe, we

Alto: Although we live beneath the cloud of greedy cor-por - a - tions we must believe we

Tenor: Although we live beneath the cloud of greedy cor-por - a - tions we must believe we

Bass: Although we live beneath the cloud of greedy cor-por - a - tions we must believe we

S: will achieve our proper li - ber - a - tion. The world of business marches on as

A: will achieve our proper li - ber - a - tion. The world of business marches on as

T: will achieve our proper li - ber - a - tion. The world of business marches on as

B: will achieve our proper li - ber - a - tion. The world of business marches on as

though it can't be halted but tyrants past have fallen down when peasants have re - volted,

though it can't be halted but tyrants past have fallen down when peasants have re - volted.

though it can't be halted but tyrants past have fallen down when peasants have re - volted

though it can't be halted but tyrants past have fallen down when peasants have re - volted,

Good-bye Gap! Good-bye Shell! Good bye Coca - Cola! To - day we save each other from our

Good-bye Gap! Good-bye Shell! Good-bye Coca - Cola! To - day we save each other from our

Good-bye Gap! Good-bye Shell! Good-bye Coca - Cola! To - day we save each other from our

Good-bye Gap! Good-bye Shell! Good-bye Coca - Cola! To - day we save each other from our

gluttonous con - trol - ler. The world was ill with wretched pain, it's creatures bound in

chains, but justice is a - live today! Co - op - er - a - tion reigns! Ha, ha, ha, ha!

chains, but justice is a - live today! Co - op - er - a - tion reigns! Ha, ha, ha, ha!

S: reigns! Ha, ha, ha! Justice is a - live today! Co - oper - ation reigns! Ha, ha! Co-oper - ation reigns!

A: reigns! Ha, ha, ha! Justice is a - live today! Co - oper - ation reigns! Ha, ha! Co -oper - ation reigns!

T: reigns! Ha, ha, ha! Justice is a - live today! Co - oper - ation reigns! Ha, ha! Co - oper - ation reigns!

B: reigns! Ha, ha, ha! Justice is a - live today! Co - oper - ation reigns! Ha, ha! Co - oper - ation reigns!

Co-operation Reigns

Although we live beneath the cloud of greed corporations,
We must believe we will achieve our proper liberation
The world of business marches on as if it can't be halted
But tyrants past have fallen down when peasants have revolted,

Goodbye GAP, Goodbye Shell, Goodbye Coka Cola
Today we save each other from our gluttonous controller
The World was ill with wretched pain, its creatures bound in chains
But justice is alive today! Co-operation reigns! Ha Ha Ha Ha

The world has been through times of good and times of rampant evil,
But nothing we have seen has made us sad beyond retrieval,
For every season cycles 'round and Winter turns to harvest
And justice rallies close again when once it was the farthest

Goodbye GAP, Goodbye Shell, Goodbye Coka Cola
Today we save each other from our gluttonous controller
The World was ill with wretched pain, its creatures bound in chains
But justice is alive today! Co-operation reigns! Ha Ha Ha Ha

We'll sing this song the day we're free from bondage to the wealthy
When streets are filled with dance and song and lives are full and healthy
But victory comes by small degrees and constant confrontation
So every time we take a step we'll sing in celebration.

Goodbye GAP, Goodbye Shell, Goodbye Coka Cola
Today we save each other from our gluttonous controller
The World was ill with wretched pain, its creatures bound in chains
But justice is alive today! Co-operation reigns! Ha Ha Ha Ha

Paul Spencer 2000

Chapter Seventeen

You can't scare me, I'm sticking to the union, 1999

During the seventeen years since the NUM Strike ended in 1985 the choir has sung on demonstrations and at benefits throughout Wales and UK.

We were at Wapping with SOGAT Print Workers, in Cheltenham supporting GCHQ, and in Blaenau Ffestiniog, North Wales, backing the quarry workers with a cast of thousands, but we were also in Sheffield supporting the forgotten trade unionists from AEU Keatons.

In Cloness, Ireland, New Year 1993, we joined a sit-in at a factory on a freezing cold morning. When the owners had the electricity and water cut off, a neighbouring factory unit connected them to their supply. It was colder in the building than outside. They gave us steaming cups of tea. Maybe it was to stop us singing.

Most of our campaigning is done in Cardiff, where we raise awareness while collecting money for trade unionists on strike, but we have been on picket lines and sung at benefits throughout Wales. We found Burton Biscuits' picket line in Cwmbran when we were returning from an Anti-Apartheid Concert at Llantarnam Arts Centre. The crowd lining the streets of Caernarfon in support of T & G Friction Dynamics clapped us as we sang our way up the hill to the town centre.

Not everyone appreciates the choir muscling in on their picket line. In 2002 the council workers went on strike. We offered our services to Unison. They were very pleased, and gave us a list of four picket lines where they wanted us to sing. We started early in the morning at Tredomen, Caerffili Council office and received our usual welcome. After the media had been there we drove off to our next appointment at

Friction Dynamics Strike, Caernarfon, north Wales, 8 June 2002

Ystrad Fawr council offices. Some pickets sang with us and asked for copies of the songs. Across the road there was a picket line outside an education office. It wasn't on our list but we thought we should give them some solidarity cheer. Flags flying, we crossed the road to join them. They were not particularly welcoming, so after our first song we asked what the situation was in the building. All of the staff had crossed the picket line apart from one woman who hadn't arrived for work. Her employers said she was off sick. The photographer hired by the union arrived. He wanted a colourful shot of the choir flags and the pickets holding placards. The choir sang while he took the photographs. As we were leaving for our next appointment a woman picket informed us that we couldn't sing and she didn't know why we had come. Arriving at our next picket line a little crushed we approached the unionists and told them we were Côr Cochion Caerdydd.

"Would you like us to sing?"

"Of course. We've been expecting you. Sandwiches and drinks will be arriving soon for your lunch, so you had better earn them."

Dover P&O Seafarers strike 1989

UNION MAID

Words and music: Woody Guthrie

There once was a union maid, who never was afraid
Of goons and ginks and company finks and the deputy sheriffs that made the raid;
She went to the union hall when a meeting it was called,
And when the company boys came round she always stood her ground.

CHORUS:
Oh, you can't scare me, I'm sticking to the union,
I'm sticking to the union, I'm sticking to the union;
Oh, you can't scare me I'm sticking to the union,
I'm sticking to the union till the day I die.

This union maid was wise to the tricks of the company spies,
She never got fooled by a company stool, she'd always organize the guys;
She always got her way when she struck for higher pay;
She'd show her card to the company guard and this is what she'd say...

A woman's struggle is hard, even with a union card;
She's got to stand on her own two feet and not be a servant of a male elite;
It's time to take a stand, keep working hand in hand,
There is a job that's got to be done, and a fight that's got to be won.

Chapter Eighteen

We'll Be Singing Songs of Freedom, 2000

Millennium year in the life of Côr Cochion Caerdydd

2000 was designated the year of peace by UNA, but passed unnoticed by the British government. The choir sang at many peace events.

At Faslane polaris base in Scotland in February, 400 picketers – half of them youngsters – held up work at the base for an hour. We were soaked to the skin and left to shiver for 24 hours, first in a queue outside the police van, then in the van, and later in an unheated cell. Despite this, we had some fun. We played cat and mouse with the police on the picket line, standing up and moving, to avoid arrest, then stopping the traffic at a different point. The police were very pleasant to us. We felt sorry for the little boys in their saturated blue uniforms. The women led the singing in one of the police stations, which was appreciated by prisoners and police. The demonstration made headline news in tabloids and broadsheets and on TV. All of us got off with a caution except Mary Millington. She appeared in court Wednesday 6th December 2000. Ray Davies went as a witness for her.

In May we supported Campaign Against the Arms Trade who were picketing British Aerospace Establishments throughout Britain on the same day that CAAT were disrupting the BAE AGM in London. Twelve of us at a BEA in Gwent caused a tailback of traffic onto the main road half a mile away, causing disruption for two miles. We held up work for twenty minutes. After the demo the choir secretary went to the toilet. She returned to find her comrades had deserted her. She was grateful to accept a lift back to the police station in a police car.

The last caravan was removed from Greenham Common in September and we sang it on its way. There were more media there, including CNN, than demonstrators. My neighbour saw me while she was on holiday in Spain.

Abergavenny Peace and Justice group invited us to sing against sanctions in Iraq in May and to launch One World Week in October. We were amazed by our reception, raising over £60 for voices in the Wilderness Iraqi Appeal on the first occasion and almost £200 in October for the Iraqi Miriam Appeal.

We have continued running workshops on local social history and internationalism in Merthyr primary schools throughout the year, funded by the European Millenium grant to Merthyr Library. The workshops are run in conjunction with banner-making lessons and creative writing workshops. A teacher at one primary school is the granddaughter of the Spanish Civil War International Brigader Will Painter. The caretaker of Rhyd y Graig Welsh Language Primary School is the son of International Brigadier Lance Rogers. This made our message far more relevant to the children.

In May we took part in a fundraising event with Dafydd Iwan, for Ysgol y Castell Welsh Language primary school in Caerffili.

Bloody Sunday in Derry, Ireland was commemorated in London in January. There is a memorial in Cathays cemetery, Cardiff to those who died or emigrated during the Great Hunger in Ireland. We had an amazing collection, raising £65 in torrential rain for a cause which could hardly be described as popular. The inappropriately-nicknamed King Billy Hotel in Newport hosted a concert to raise money for the tour of a Sinn Fein speaker in a bar painted orange, white, and green with a tricolour on the wall and with the barmaid dressed in traditional Irish costume.

Until the intifada (uprising) which started in October 2000, the choir supported Palestine Solidarity Campaign Cymru every eight weeks on the Hayes for Palestinian Right To Return Home. We also

Merthyr Tydfil Primary Schools. Local history in song, stories, poetry, and the tradition of banner-making. Ynys Owen Primary School

Merthyr Tydfil Primary Schools. Local history project with banners.

supported the annual sponsored walk for the Women's Cooperative in Al Berah, West Bank which raised about £200. In October we supported the Appeal of Samar and Jawad, two Palestinians imprisoned on the charge of bombing the Israeli Embassy. The case was well-covered by the media. The annual Palestinian Social was held in the Temple of Peace this year. Since the intifada started, the choir has been at the Hayes twice a week supporting PSC by singing as they collected signatures asking for a UN peace-keeping force and an embargo on armaments to and from Israel. Over a thousand letters signed by people in Cardiff city centre have also been sent to MPs, MEPs and the National Assembly for Wales. Thousands of pounds collected in Cardiff have been

taken to a hospitals in Gaza and the West Bank.

Racism has been a major issue, particularly since the government started to disperse asylum seekers in July 2000. We had already been involved with the plight of three young Turkish men who were beaten up in a racist attack in Cwmbran. The choir supported a demonstration at Newport Police Station demanding a trial. An Indonesian man was murdered in the grounds of the Royal Gwent Hospital, almost opposite the police station, the night before the demonstration about the Turks. A vigil held on the spot where the Indonesian was attacked was led by the choir. We sang twice a week at the Hayes, Cardiff while giving out leaflets to raise awareness and understanding about asylum seekers.

Welsh self-awareness came to a head when the Welsh were left off the census form. This has been covered by the media, particularly the *Western Mail*. The census form was burned outside the Welsh Office. At first it wouldn't light then the burning paper was blown toward the children causing Myrla to dance on it. She hopes that wasn't caught on camara.

Welsh history was remembered on Dic Penderyn Day in August. It always seems to be the hottest day of the year.

Protesting against new Terrorism Act. Welsh National Assembly,
October 2000

The 600 anniversary of Owain Glyndŵr's Parliament was celebrated in Machynlleth in September 2000. The fuel picket prevented most people getting there. English-speaking, right-wing nationalists were in the majority.

Llywelyn Ein Llyw Olaf, Prince of Wales was commemorated in Cilmeri in December. Macs, wellies and a torch were the order of the day as usual. It is always an enjoyable occasion and well worth facing the elements to attend. Community pub singing is rare these days so the evening at the Prince Llywelyn is a real bonus.

One of the most pleasurable highlights of the year was singing with and for Desmond Tutu, retired Archbishop of South Africa in the grand old City Hall in Cardiff. He wasn't looking very well but we were delighted to renew our acquaintance. The choir first sang for him in 1986 during the dark days of apartheid when he was made a Freeman of Merthyr Tydfil. When he came to Cardiff in 1998 to receive an honourary degree from the University of Wales he sang 'Ncosi Sikalali', the South African national anthem with us.

Nestle received our attention when they sponsored the Hayes Island Snack Bar. The sponsorship advertisement was removed within the first week of our campaign but the sponsorship continues. The choir now wanders from place to place looking for somewhere PC and cheap to eat.

May day saw a fun day from young people raising awareness about the Terrorism Bill and globalisation on Queen street. Students joined the demo at the National Assembly about the Terrorism Act in October. We have raised awareness about the Ilisu Dam which will destroy hundreds of Kurdish villages. A Spanish Civil War plaque was unveiled on the Plaid Cymru Office in Llanelli, and a bridge in Maerdy was named after Frank Owen, International Brigadier. Both plaques deserve a paragraph, but that would mean starting another page. Annual events such as International Women's Day in were celebrated. The Street Music Festival in Manchester was a very enjoyable occasion. We also renewed old friendships at Fête de l'Humanité in Paris. Nicaragua Solidarity, Ciwba Cymru, and Liberty continued to receive our support three or four times during the year. This year we also supported the campaign to cancel world debt organised by Jubilee 2000 et al about every eight weeks.

The year 2000 started with a concert inside Campsfield Detention Centre for Asylum Seekers and ended in December 2000 with the choir returned to their proper station – outside with the hoi polloi.

Cilmeri, December 2000. Commemorating the assassination of Llywelyn ein Llyw Olaf, the last Prince of Wales.

Songs of Freedom

Words by Ann Marie Fearon and other members of Côr Cochion Caerdydd
Music: 'Hymns and Arias' by Max Boyce.

The miners, with their sweat and pain, they paid the price of coal,
And then the Tories closed the pits, put thousands on the dole;
But the lads of Tower colliery had faith in what they knew,
Swore they'd run the pits themselves,
And show what working folk can do.

And they were singing, songs of freedom,
And peace and justice and workers power.

SONGS OF FREEDOM

SONGS OF FREEDOM

Based on an idea by Ann Marie Fearon and Lyn Mererid 1997
Tune: 'Hymns and Arias', by Max Boyce

1. You've heard about South Africa and the cruel Apartheid laws,
And how a man called Mandela spoke out in freedom's cause;
Spent twenty-seven years in jail for his courageous stand,
At last he was released and now he's President of the land,
   And he's still singing, songs of freedom,
   And peace and justice, and human rights.

2. The miners with their sweat and pain, they paid the price of coal,
And then the Tories closed the pits, put thousands on the dole;
But the lads of Tower Colliery had faith in what they knew,
Swore they'd run the pit themselves and show what working folk can do,
   And now they're singing, songs of freedom,
   And peace and justice, and workers' power.

3. Now the fight for women's suffrage was bitter, long and hard;
In Holloway jail they sang this song -
   "March! March! Swing we along ..." out in the exercise yard;
And Ethel Smythe, who wrote the song, imprisoned there as well,
Conducted with her toothbrush from the window of her cell,
   For they were singing, songs of freedom,
   And peace and justice, and women's rights.

4. Now we've won a Welsh Assembly and it's taken quite a time,
And it's been an uphill struggle since 1979;
But the country chose democracy at the 11th hour,
Now Hague and all the Torys have to bow to people power.
   And we were singing songs of freedom,
   And peace and justice, and Yes for Wales.

5. The Welsh Assembly leadership is in a fine old mess
Since Ron resigned from office and was hounded by the press.
The powers that be got Michael by fixing as they can,
But we the people know - that Rhodri Morgan is our man.
   Because he's singing songs of freedom
   And peace and justice One Member One Vote!

6. They say that General Pinochet is just a frail old man (Aah),
Never meant no harm to no-one - well, believe that if you can!
He had thousands killed and tortured to protect the wealthy few,
But now he knows that generals can get arrested too!
   That's why we're singing songs of freedom
   And peace and justice. - Throw away the key!

7. We arranged a May Day concert with the Chorale Populaire,
But Myrla, Anne-Marie and Lyn they didn't quite know where.
Then up the Eiffle Tower, Dave was loth to make a move,
While poor old Dawn and Cheryl were imprisoned in the Louvre.
   But they were singing songs of freedom
   And peace and justice and C'est Paris!

8. To the European Parliament we went one winter day
To call for full employment, equal rights and decent pay.
One comrade broke her bottles when she took a painful trip
But free whisky tasting sessions raised our spirits on the ship.
   For we were singing songs of freedom
   And peace and justice and jobs for all!

9. Wendy our glorious leader was by the Euro bar
When a fellow chorister took a step too far.
The coffee she was carrying burnt our Wendy's chest.
Now red but not defeated she can sing without her vest.
   And she was singing, fetch me cold water
   And tissue paper and here's your note!

10. Our Choir was formed in '83 and it's going strong today
Supporting those in struggle both at home and far away;
So why not come and join us in the fight that must be won
For a world more just and equal, and more human, and more fun!
   And we'll be singing, songs of freedom,
   And peace and justice, for evermore.
   The whole world singing, songs of freedom
   And peace and justice, for evermore.

Chapter Nineteen

We are a gentle, angry people
Lesbian and Gay rights, 2001

In keeping with their principles, Côr Cochion have supported campaigns for lesbian and gay rights, and against homophobia.

On Saturday 2nd September 2000, the choir sang in Sophia Gardens, Cardiff, at the Lesbian and Gay Mardi Gras. Initially word got around that there would be a gay pride march through town and the choir intended to sing to support this march. Nearer the time it was discovered that there would not be a march, so some choir members came along after the street sing to the Mardi Gras, where we sang.

The choir also supported the Welsh campaign in 2001 to repeal Section 28, a homophobic act passed in 1988 under the Tory government, which has now been repealed by the Scottish Parliament. We sang with protestors outside the City Hall, and these are a sample of some of the songs (adapted from our present repertoire):

Lestbian and Gay Pride march, London, 1998

Our own democracy (adapted from an Irish song)

Cold and dark the morning, standing here as one,
The old law needs repealing, our struggle has begun.
The people are together, we shall be free,
In this land our homeland, our own democracy.

Oh straights and gays, come rally, rally to our cause,
And seek the abolition of homophobic laws.
Let us open every eye, let the people see
What this land, our homeland, means to you and
me.

How far must we travel till our journey's done?
How long must we struggle till the fight is won?
May we have equality, may we live to see
Section 28 repealed in this new century.

Songs of Freedom
Tune; 'Hymns and Arias', Max Boyce)

You've heard about the Tories and their homophobic laws,
And how lesbians and gays have suffered under their clause.
Why should we have Clause 28?
Why keep us underground?
Within this new millennium let equality abound.

And we'll be singing songs of freedom,
And peace and justice and rights for all,
The whole world singing songs of freedom
And peace and justice forever more.

At this rally, the choir also sang the song 'We Are a Gentle, Angry People' by American singer-songwriter Holly Near, which she had first composed in dedication to Harvey Milk, gay mayor of San Francisco, who was assassinated in a homophobic attack in 1978.

In January 2001, the choir sent a donation to Stonewall Cymru, which has recently been set up in Wales, and is involved in campaigns and support for the lesbian, gay and bisexual community in Wales. It is also involved in lobbying the Welsh Assembly to fight against discrimination and homophobia, and to work towards scrapping Section 28 in Wales.

Wendy Lewis of Côr Cochion Caerdydd and Manchester Community Choir have done a recent arrangement of the song, 'Something Inside So Strong', written by Labi Siffre, a gay black poet from Wales, and this is included in our repertoire.

*Lesbian and Gay Pride march, London, 1998.
Banner from Cardiff*

WHY ARE WE VICTIMS?

Sean Dudson arr Joa

Why Are We Victims?

Why are we victims? Why are we abused?
Why are we victims chosen by you?

What are you scared of? Why are you afraid?
Why can't you accept that people are G.A.Y.

You accuse us with lies while truth is denied.
You accuse us with lies, with lies.

You torture our minds. You target our lives.
You torture our minds, our minds.

You cannot hide us, you cannot hide us from view.
You cannot hide us, hide us from view.

We are your equal, We are good as you.
We are your equal, as good as you.

Chapter Twenty

No fascist shall defeat us, 2002
Anti-fascism, Anti-racism, 1983–2002

The attack on a synagogue in Swansea was announced on BBC Radio 4 news at 6 p.m. on Friday 12th July 2002. Immediately, frantic calls began whistling down the phone lines as the choir called each other and called the Anti-Nazi League. They also called the organisation the choir was booked to sing for on Saturday, 13th July 2002 to cancel the booking.

This is a Fascist Free Zone. Caerffili, South Wales, 1995

The ANL contact in Cardiff gave us a number in Swansea and then went out to a meeting. Intermittently throughout the evening we called the Swansea number, without success. Meanwhile the choir made a definite decision to go to Swansea. Lifts had to be arranged for choir members from all over Cardiff and the South Wales Valleys. We prepared placards and a petition.

At 10pm we eventually made contact with Swansea ANL, and they arranged that we meet to petition the community at the pedestrianised cross roads in the City centre. The ANL hadn't heard about the attack on the synagogue. They were organising into the early hours of the morning. The last phone call they made to their members was at 1.30 a.m., but nobody complained.

They were grateful that they had been alerted. They wanted to show the Jewish community in Swansea the strength of feeling there was against the Nazi BNP and all other racists.

On a beautiful summer morning, the choir joined over twenty members of the ANL who were informing shoppers about the attack on the synagogue. Young and old were queuing up to sign the petition. They were very angry that racism had come to their city.

A young man on a motorbike sat quietly watching and listening. He then introduced himself as the BNP representative in Swansea. He was at pains to inform us that this attack was the work of mindless thugs and that the BNP is a responsible and legitimate political party that does not participate in or condone acts of vandalism. This is the acceptable face of Nazism that the BNP is now presenting to the British public. Unfortunately many people in the north of England have been taken in by smooth talk and easy answers to poverty, unemployment and poor housing, as the German people were before the Second World War.

In Swansea the majority still remember what Nazism is, but we can't be complacent. Racist attacks are increasing in Wales and we had a murder in Newport in 2000.

The BNP held a party on a farm outside Welshpool in August 2001, to the disgust of local people. The ANL supporters, including the choir, were prevented by the police from getting within a mile of this gathering. The police penned in the ANL on a grass bank outside the town.

Ray Davies painting out Combat 18 in Caerffili. Dave Hill's poster explains that '1' stands for the letter 'A' for Adolf, and '8' stands for the letter 'H' for Hitler

The choir crossed the police cordon into Welshpool, looking like a strange group of old people and one younger blind person with her youthful carer. I was going to write that we passed as ordinary shoppers but that is unlikely. The teenage children of choir members held a meeting a few years ago to decide what should be done about their unruly parents.

Once we were in Welshpool and started singing and giving out leaflets, the police came rushing along the road to try to stop us, but the local people sitting outside a pub and shoppers were on our side. They were happy to accept the leaflets and enjoyed the singing. At that point the police decided that we were harmless and left us alone. Later in the day a march through the town was prevented by the police so the choir staged there own slow march down the centre of the town, holding up the police vehicles. A number of members were arrested.

From the beginning, the choir could be relied upon to stand up and fight wherever racism or fascism reared its ugly head. We have supported Anti-Apartheid, the Anti-Nazi league and the short lived Anti-Racist Alliance. We went to London after swastikas defaced a Jewish Cemetery, and were the first to offer support to the Jewish community in Cardiff when gravestones were damaged. We petitioned against the BNP candidate in Ely, Cardiff. The choir went to Caerffili and painted out the racist graffiti of Combat 18 on shops and banks.

The money collected in Swansea July 2002 was donated to the newly-founded Welsh branch of Searchlight.

The Choir with the ANL protesting against the synagogue attack by the BNP in Swansea, 13 July, 2002

ANL protest at synagogue attack

IN SWANSEA city centre last Saturday people were queuing up to sign a petition opposing the neo-Nazis who desecrated the synagogue in Fynnons Road, Swansea, by daubing Nazi symbols on the walls, breaking windows and destroying ancient manuscripts.

The Anti-Nazi League handed out leaflets and collected signatures while Cor Cochion Caerdydd (The Cardiff Reds Choir) sang songs against racism.

The attack was similar to another attack on a north London synagogue in April.

o The metropolitan police last week charged a man with the murder and dismemberment of a gay trainee rabbi. They suspect this may be a hate crime.

The butchered remains of Andreas Hinz were found less than a mile from a north London gay pub he was last seen leaving on 3 July.

The whole wide world around

Words by Tom Glazer
Music by Hans Hessler
Choral arrangement by Johann Sebastian Bach

Because we all are comrades, wherever we may be,
One union shall unite us, forever proud and free.
No fascist shall defeat us, no nation strike us down.
All those who toil shall greet us the whole wide world around.

My comrades are all others, forever hand in hand.
Wherever people struggle, there is my native land.
My comrade's fears are my fears, I shall not let them down.
My comrade's tears are my tears, the whole wide world around.

Let every voice be thunder, let every heart be stone.
Until all tyrants perish, our work shall not be done.
Let every pain be token; the lost years shall be found.
Let slavery's chain be broken, the whole wide around.

THE WHOLE WIDE WORLD AROUND

Choral arrangement by Johann Sebastian Bach

This melody was a favorite of Bach's, and he used it in various choral works. It is known as one of the most beautiful four-part arrangements in musical literature. The lyrics are dedicated to the World Federation of Trade Unions.

Subscribers to *Stand up and Sing*

Paul Ambeliotis	New Communist Party
Dr Robin & Leela Attfield	United Nations Association, etc
Paul Barrett	New Communist Party
Jean Bryant	Campaign for Nuclear Disarmament
Ann Conway	Palestine Solidarity Campaign, etc
Diane Corker	Côr Cochion Caerdydd Member
Norma Couper	Côr Cochion Caerdydd Member
Ann Cox	Cardiff Councillor, Labour
George & Jean Crabb	Ex Services CND
Olwen Davies	Campaign for Nuclear Disarmament, etc
Rose Dentus	Nicaragua Solidarity, etc
Neil Donovan	Friends of the Earth
Dennis Eady	Liberty
Dr Keith Flett	London Socialist Historians Group
Ann Foley	Palestine Solidarity Campaign
Barbara Foxworthy	United Nations Association, etc
Rev. Chris Gillham	Palestine Solidarity
Teresa & Julian Goss	South Wales Coalition to Stop the War
Sue Hendrickson	Palestine Solidarity
Bob Hill	
David Hill	Côr Cochion Caerdydd Member. Coun. Labour
Kate Howard	Calder Valley Voices
Dr. H. G. Alun Hughes	
Stuart Hyslop	National Union of Rail, Maritime & Transport Workers
Margaret Innocent	Côr Cochion Caerdydd Member
Alun Jones	Ex-Côr Cochion Caerdydd Member
Transport & General W.U.	Friction Dynamics Caernarfon
Sue Jones-Davies	Singer. Campaign for Nuclear Disarmament
Joan Judson	Palestine Solidarity Campaign, CND, T.U. Labour
Peter Keelan	Campaign for Nuclear Disarmament, etc
Phillip Kingston	Campaign Against the Arms Trade etc
Rt. Hon. Neil Kinnock	Vice President, European Commission
John Lent	Communist Party of Britain
Sue Lent	Côr Cochion Caerdydd Member. Coun. Labour, Cardiff
Clare Leonard	Ex-Côr Cochion Caerdydd Member
Comrade Olwen of Dolgellau	Côr Cochion Caerdydd Member
Wendy Lewis	Musical Director, Côr Cochion Caerdydd
Ken & Joyce Llewellyn	Campaign for Nuclear Disarmament
Tim Lockhart	Amnesty International, etc
Ann Lukes	Campaign for Nuclear Disarmament
Esther Macloed	Palestine Forum. Friends of Sabeel
Colin Matthews	Ex-Côr Cochion Caerdydd Member
Michael McPhillips	
Mary Millington	Yellow Gate. Greenham Common. Ex-Côr Cochion
Teresa Mitchell	Medical Foundation for Victims of Torture
Julie Morgan MP	Labour Party, Cardiff
Cymtha Morris	Campaign for Nuclear Disarmament
Dr. Miranda Morton	Writer
Chris Newman	Ex-Côr Cochion Caerdydd Member
Dorothy Nind	Anti-Poll Tax Campaign. CND, Anti-Apartheid, etc
Tyrone O'Sullivan	Tower Colliery
David Owen	Public & Commercial Services Union, Liverpool
Linda Price	Chernobyl Children's Project. Amnesty International
Alon Prytherch	
Tim & Judy Richards	Welsh Republicans
Sonia Robbins	Palestine Solidarity
Beryl Rubens	Palestine Solidarity Campaign. CND
Annie Smith	Birmingham Clarion Singers
Rod & Jill Stallard	Campaign for Nuclear Disarmament Wales/Cymru
Jane Tallents	Trident Ploughshares
Helen Thomas	
Ruth Thomas	Ex-Côr Cochion Caerdydd Member
National Union of Mineworkers	South Wales Area
National Union of Mineworkers	Tower Colliery Lodge
Marie Walsh	Côr Cochion Caerdydd Member
Rod Walters	Palestine Solidarity Campaign
Bob Watson	Campaign for Nuclear Disarmament
Lindsey Whittle	Leader, Caerffili Borough Council, Plaid Cymru
Aerfen Whittle	
Selwyn Williams	Cymru Ciwba
Hywel Williams MP	Plaid Cymru, Caernarfon
Mary Wines	
Leanne Wood AM	Assembly Member, National Assembly for Wales
Eurig Wyn ASE MEP	Plaid Cymru